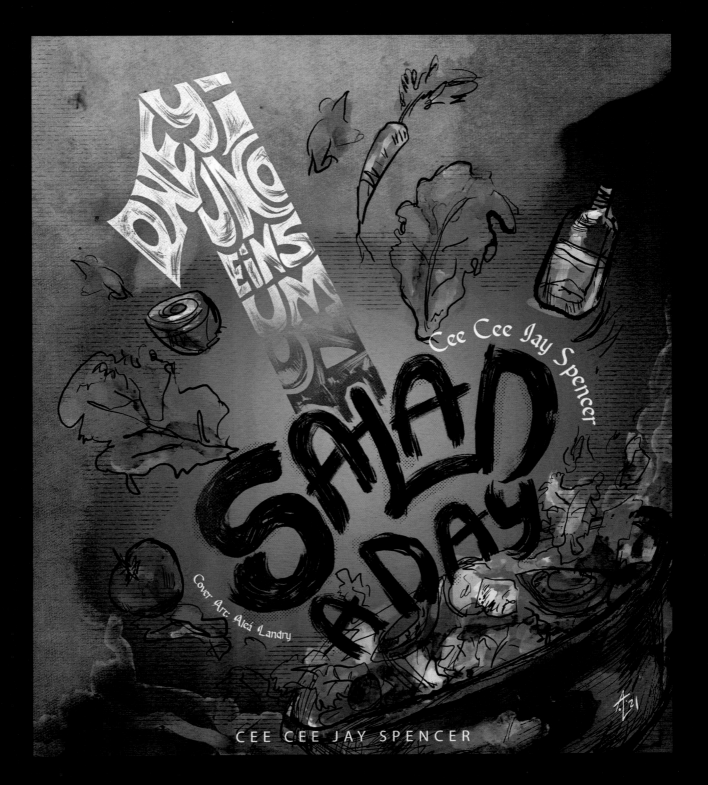

The *One Salad A Day* book was written to encourage
the art of salad making for fun and enjoyment. I am
stating that I am not a professional cook, nutritionist,
medical professional, or food critic. Any question about
the food choices you want to use, ask a professional.

To order additional copies of this book, contact:
Xlibris
844-714-8691
www.Xlibris.com
Orders@Xlibris.com

ISBN: Softcover   978-1-6698-0152-8
         Hardcover   978-1-6698-0153-5
         EBook   978-1-6698-0151-1

Library of Congress Control Number: 2022900643

Print information available on the last page.

Rev. date: 01/12/2022

Take an adventure with *One Salad A Day*. Because your mind and body work together in concert, the importance of great foods is paramount. *One Salad A Day* will encourage you to create your own salad to share with people in your life's circle and so many others. Create with boldness and be excited about having a contribution of what you think tastes great and ultimately will assist you on your journey of better health. The variations of salads that you create with your food choices will be endless. So create one salad a day, enjoy the experience, journal the path you took, and let others know the fun you had along the way.

Acknowledgment

To the Creator of life, I give thanks!

Creation Page

Name of salad (optional): _____

Popular items chosen: _____

Mix and match salad fixings: _____

_____

_____

_____

_____

_____

_____

_____

Create your own salad dressing: _____

_____

_____

_____

_____

_____

_____

Journal your thoughts: _____

_____

_____

_____

_____

_____

_____

_____

Encouragement: Think of yourself as an artist creating a salad that will draw in your family and friends. Bring alive your passion for food and feel joy as you prepare one salad a day.

Creation Page

Name of salad (optional): _____

Popular items chosen: _____

Mix and match salad fixings: _____
_____
_____
_____
_____
_____
_____
_____

Create your own salad dressing: _____
_____
_____
_____
_____
_____
_____
_____

Journal your thoughts: _____
_____
_____
_____
_____
_____
_____
_____

Creation Page

Name of salad (optional): _____

Popular items chosen: _____

Mix and match salad fixings: _____

_____

_____

_____

_____

_____

_____

_____

Create your own salad dressing: _____

_____

_____

_____

_____

_____

_____

_____

Journal your thoughts: _____

_____

_____

_____

_____

_____

_____

_____

Creation Page

Name of salad (optional): _____

Popular items chosen: _____

Mix and match salad fixings: _____
_____
_____
_____
_____
_____
_____
_____

Create your own salad dressing: _____
_____
_____
_____
_____
_____
_____

Journal your thoughts: _____
_____
_____
_____
_____
_____
_____

Creation Page

Name of salad (optional): _____

Popular items chosen: _____

Mix and match salad fixings: _____

_____

_____

_____

_____

_____

_____

_____

Create your own salad dressing: _____

_____

_____

_____

_____

_____

_____

Journal your thoughts: _____

_____

_____

_____

_____

_____

_____

Creation Page

Name of salad (optional): _____

Popular items chosen: _____

Mix and match salad fixings: _____

_____

_____

_____

_____

_____

_____

_____

Create your own salad dressing: _____

_____

_____

_____

_____

_____

_____

_____

Journal your thoughts: _____

_____

_____

_____

_____

_____

_____

_____

Creation Page

Name of salad (optional): _____

Popular items chosen: _____

Mix and match salad fixings: _____
_____
_____
_____
_____
_____
_____
_____

Create your own salad dressing: _____
_____
_____
_____
_____
_____
_____

Journal your thoughts: _____
_____
_____
_____
_____
_____
_____
_____

Creation Page

Name of salad (optional): _____

Popular items chosen: _____

Mix and match salad fixings: _____

_____

_____

_____

_____

_____

_____

_____

Create your own salad dressing: _____

_____

_____

_____

_____

_____

_____

Journal your thoughts: _____

_____

_____

_____

_____

_____

_____

_____

Creation Page

Name of salad (optional): _____

Popular items chosen: _____

Mix and match salad fixings: _____

_____

_____

_____

_____

_____

_____

_____

Create your own salad dressing: _____

_____

_____

_____

_____

_____

_____

_____

Journal your thoughts: _____

_____

_____

_____

_____

_____

_____

_____

Creation Page

Name of salad (optional): _____

Popular items chosen: _____

Mix and match salad fixings: _____
_____
_____
_____
_____
_____
_____
_____

Create your own salad dressing: _____
_____
_____
_____
_____
_____
_____

Journal your thoughts: _____
_____
_____
_____
_____
_____
_____

Creation Page

Name of salad (optional): _____

Popular items chosen: _____

Mix and match salad fixings: _____

_____

_____

_____

_____

_____

_____

_____

Create your own salad dressing: _____

_____

_____

_____

_____

_____

_____

Journal your thoughts: _____

_____

_____

_____

_____

_____

_____

Creation Page

Name of salad (optional): _____

Popular items chosen: _____

Mix and match salad fixings: _____

_____

_____

_____

_____

_____

_____

_____

Create your own salad dressing: _____

_____

_____

_____

_____

_____

_____

_____

Journal your thoughts: _____

_____

_____

_____

_____

_____

_____

_____

Creation Page

Name of salad (optional): _____

Popular items chosen: _____

Mix and match salad fixings: _____
_____
_____
_____
_____
_____
_____
_____

Create your own salad dressing: _____
_____
_____
_____
_____
_____
_____
_____

Journal your thoughts: _____
_____
_____
_____
_____
_____
_____
_____

Creation Page

Name of salad (optional): _____

Popular items chosen: _____

Mix and match salad fixings: _____
_____
_____
_____
_____
_____
_____
_____

Create your own salad dressing: _____
_____
_____
_____
_____
_____
_____

Journal your thoughts: _____
_____
_____
_____
_____
_____
_____

Creation Page

Name of salad (optional): _____

Popular items chosen: _____

Mix and match salad fixings: _____

_____

_____

_____

_____

_____

_____

_____

Create your own salad dressing: _____

_____

_____

_____

_____

_____

_____

_____

Journal your thoughts: _____

_____

_____

_____

_____

_____

_____

_____

Creation Page

Name of salad (optional): _____

Popular items chosen: _____

Mix and match salad fixings: _____
_____
_____
_____
_____
_____
_____
_____

Create your own salad dressing: _____
_____
_____
_____
_____
_____
_____

Journal your thoughts: _____
_____
_____
_____
_____
_____
_____

Creation Page

Name of salad (optional): _____

Popular items chosen: _____

Mix and match salad fixings: _____

_____

_____

_____

_____

_____

_____

_____

Create your own salad dressing: _____

_____

_____

_____

_____

_____

_____

_____

Journal your thoughts: _____

_____

_____

_____

_____

_____

_____

_____

Creation Page

Name of salad (optional): _____

Popular items chosen: _____

Mix and match salad fixings: _____

_____

_____

_____

_____

_____

_____

_____

Create your own salad dressing: _____

_____

_____

_____

_____

_____

_____

Journal your thoughts: _____

_____

_____

_____

_____

_____

_____

Creation Page

Name of salad (optional): _____

Popular items chosen: _____

Mix and match salad fixings: _____
_____
_____
_____
_____
_____
_____
_____

Create your own salad dressing: _____
_____
_____
_____
_____
_____
_____
_____
_____

Journal your thoughts: _____
_____
_____
_____
_____
_____
_____
_____

Creation Page

Name of salad (optional): _____

Popular items chosen: _____

Mix and match salad fixings: _____
_____
_____
_____
_____
_____
_____
_____

Create your own salad dressing: _____
_____
_____
_____
_____
_____
_____

Journal your thoughts: _____
_____
_____
_____
_____
_____
_____

Creation Page

Name of salad (optional): _____

Popular items chosen: _____

Mix and match salad fixings: _____

_____

_____

_____

_____

_____

_____

_____

Create your own salad dressing: _____

_____

_____

_____

_____

_____

_____

_____

Journal your thoughts: _____

_____

_____

_____

_____

_____

_____

_____

Creation Page

Name of salad (optional): _____

Popular items chosen: _____

Mix and match salad fixings: _____

_____

_____

_____

_____

_____

_____

_____

Create your own salad dressing: _____

_____

_____

_____

_____

_____

_____

_____

Journal your thoughts: _____

_____

_____

_____

_____

_____

_____

Creation Page

Name of salad (optional): _____

Popular items chosen: _____

Mix and match salad fixings: _____
_____
_____
_____
_____
_____
_____
_____

Create your own salad dressing: _____
_____
_____
_____
_____
_____
_____

Journal your thoughts: _____
_____
_____
_____
_____
_____
_____
_____

Creation Page

Name of salad (optional): _____

Popular items chosen: _____

Mix and match salad fixings: _____

_____

_____

_____

_____

_____

_____

_____

Create your own salad dressing: _____

_____

_____

_____

_____

_____

_____

_____

Journal your thoughts: _____

_____

_____

_____

_____

_____

_____

Creation Page

Name of salad (optional): _____

Popular items chosen: _____

Mix and match salad fixings: _____

_____

_____

_____

_____

_____

_____

_____

Create your own salad dressing: _____

_____

_____

_____

_____

_____

_____

_____

Journal your thoughts: _____

_____

_____

_____

_____

_____

_____

Creation Page

Name of salad (optional): _____

Popular items chosen: _____

Mix and match salad fixings: _____

_____

_____

_____

_____

_____

_____

_____

Create your own salad dressing: _____

_____

_____

_____

_____

_____

_____

Journal your thoughts: _____

_____

_____

_____

_____

_____

_____

Creation Page

Name of salad (optional): _____

Popular items chosen: _____

Mix and match salad fixings: _____
_____
_____
_____
_____
_____
_____
_____

Create your own salad dressing: _____
_____
_____
_____
_____
_____
_____

Journal your thoughts: _____
_____
_____
_____
_____
_____
_____

Creation Page

Name of salad (optional): _____

Popular items chosen: _____

Mix and match salad fixings: _____

_____

_____

_____

_____

_____

_____

_____

Create your own salad dressing: _____

_____

_____

_____

_____

_____

_____

_____

Journal your thoughts: _____

_____

_____

_____

_____

_____

_____

_____

Creation Page

Name of salad (optional): _____

Popular items chosen: _____

Mix and match salad fixings: _____
_____
_____
_____
_____
_____
_____
_____

Create your own salad dressing: _____
_____
_____
_____
_____
_____
_____

Journal your thoughts: _____
_____
_____
_____
_____
_____
_____

Creation Page

Name of salad (optional): _____

Popular items chosen: _____

Mix and match salad fixings: _____

_____

_____

_____

_____

_____

_____

_____

Create your own salad dressing: _____

_____

_____

_____

_____

_____

_____

_____

Journal your thoughts: _____

_____

_____

_____

_____

_____

_____

One Salad A Day Food Choices

1. Lettuce
2. Tomatoes
3. Cucumbers
4. Berries
5. Fruits
6. Olives
7. Cranberries
8. Raisins
9. Nuts
10. Vegetables
11. Beans
12. Beets
13. Peas
14. Onions
15. Garlic
16. Tuna
17. Chicken
18. Turkey
19. Fish
20. Eggs
21. Cheeses

Salad items are not limited to the suggestions above. The choices as you create your own salad will be limitless.

Items can be fresh or canned, sliced, diced, and or shredded. Seasonings span a wide array of choices too, so have fun while creating. Meat and/or fish of any kind must be cooked before placing it on the salad.

Printed in the United States
by Baker & Taylor Publisher Services